The Poetry of Algernon Charles Swinburne

VOLUME VIII - STUDIES IN SONG

Algernon Charles Swinburne was born on April 5th, 1837, in London, into a wealthy Northumbrian family. He was educated at Eton and at Balliol College, Oxford, but did not complete a degree.

In 1860 Swinburne published two verse dramas but achieved his first literary success in 1865 with Atalanta in Calydon, written in the form of classical Greek tragedy. The following year "Poems and Ballads" brought him instant notoriety. He was now identified with "indecent" themes and the precept of art for art's sake.

Although he produced much after this success in general his popularity and critical reputation declined. The most important qualities of Swinburne's work are an intense lyricism, his intricately extended and evocative imagery, metrical virtuosity, rich use of assonance and alliteration, and bold, complex rhythms.

Swinburne's physical appearance was small, frail, and plagued by several other oddities of physique and temperament. Throughout the 1860s and 1870s he drank excessively and was prone to accidents that often left him bruised, bloody, or unconscious. Until his forties he suffered intermittent physical collapses that necessitated removal to his parents' home while he recovered.

Throughout his career Swinburne also published literary criticism of great worth. His deep knowledge of world literatures contributed to a critical style rich in quotation, allusion, and comparison. He is particularly noted for discerning studies of Elizabethan dramatists and of many English and French poets and novelists. As well he was a noted essayist and wrote two novels.

In 1879, Swinburne's friend and literary agent, Theodore Watts-Dunton, intervened during a time when Swinburne was dangerously ill. Watts-Dunton isolated Swinburne at a suburban home in Putney and gradually weaned him from alcohol, former companions and many other habits as well.

Much of his poetry in this period may be inferior but some individual poems are exceptional; "By the North Sea," "Evening on the Broads," "A Nympholept," "The Lake of Gaube," and "Neap-Tide."

Swinburne lived another thirty years with Watts-Dunton. He denied Swinburne's friends access to him, controlled the poet's money, and restricted his activities. It is often quoted that 'he saved the man but killed the poet'.

Swinburne died on April 10th, 1909 at the age of seventy-two.

Index of Contents

SONG FOR THE CENTENARY OF WALTER SAVAGE LANDOR

BORN JANUARY 30TH, 1775. DIED SEPTEMBER 17TH, 1864

There is delight in singing, though none hear
Beside the singer: and there is delight
In praising, though the praiser sit alone
And see the praised far off him, far above.
LANDOR.

DEDICATION

TO MRS. LYNN LINTON

Daughter in spirit elect and consecrate
By love and reverence of the Olympian sire
Whom I too loved and worshipped, seeing so great,
And found so gracious toward my long desire
To bid that love in song before his gate
Sound, and my lute be loyal to his lyre,
To none save one it now may dedicate
Song's new burnt-offering on a century's pyre.
And though the gift be light
As ashes in men's sight,
Left by the flame of no ethereal fire,
Yet, for his worthier sake
Than words are worthless, take
This wreath of words ere yet their hour expire:
So, haply, from some heaven above,
He, seeing, may set next yours my sacrifice of love.

May 24, 1880.

SONG FOR THE CENTENARY OF WALTER SAVAGE LANDOR

I

Five years beyond an hundred years have seen
Their winters, white as faith's and age's hue,
Melt, smiling through brief tears that broke between,
And hope's young conquering colours reared anew,
Since, on the day whose edge for kings made keen
Smote sharper once than ever storm-wind blew,
A head predestined for the girdling green
That laughs at lightning all the seasons through,
Nor frost or change can sunder
Its crown untouched of thunder
Leaf from least leaf of all its leaves that grew
Alone for brows too bold
For storm to sear of old,
Elect to shine in time's eternal view,
Rose on the verge of radiant life
Between the winds and sunbeams mingling love with strife.

II

The darkling day that gave its bloodred birth
To Milton's white republic undefiled
That might endure so few fleet years on earth
Bore in him likewise as divine a child;
But born not less for crowns of love and mirth,
Of palm and myrtle passionate and mild,
The leaf that girds about with gentler girth
The brow steel-bound in battle, and the wild
Soft spray that flowers above
The flower-soft hair of love;
And the white lips of wayworn winter smiled
And grew serene as spring's
When with stretched clouds like wings
Or wings like drift of snow-clouds massed and piled
The godlike giant, softening, spread
A shadow of stormy shelter round the new-born head.

III

And o'er it brightening bowed the wild-haired hour,

And touched his tongue with honey and with fire,
And breathed between his lips the note of power
That makes of all the winds of heaven a lyre
Whose strings are stretched from topmost peaks that tower
To softest springs of waters that suspire,
With sounds too dim to shake the lowliest flower
Breathless with hope and dauntless with desire:
And bright before his face
That Hour became a Grace,
As in the light of their Athenian quire
When the Hours before the sun
And Graces were made one,
Called by sweet Love down from the aerial gyre
By one dear name of natural joy,
To bear on her bright breast from heaven a heaven-born boy.

IV

Ere light could kiss the little lids in sunder
Or love could lift them for the sun to smite,
His fiery birth-star as a sign of wonder
Had risen, perplexing the presageful night
With shadow and glory around her sphere and under
And portents prophesying by sound and sight;
And half the sound was song and half was thunder,
And half his life of lightning, half of light:
And in the soft clenched hand
Shone like a burning brand
A shadowy sword for swordless fields of fight,
Wrought only for such lord
As so may wield the sword
That all things ill be put to fear and flight
Even at the flash and sweep and gleam
Of one swift stroke beheld but in a shuddering dream.

V

Like the sun's rays that blind the night's wild beasts
The sword of song shines as the swordsman sings;
From the west wind's verge even to the arduous east's
The splendour of the shadow that it flings
Makes fire and storm in heaven above the feasts
Of men fulfilled with food of evil things;
Strikes dumb the lying and hungering lips of priests,
Smites dead the slaying and ravening hands of kings;
Turns dark the lamp's hot light,

And turns the darkness bright
As with the shadow of dawn's reverberate wings;
And far before its way
Heaven, yearning toward the day,
Shines with its thunder and round its lightning rings;
And never hand yet earlier played
With that keen sword whose hilt is cloud, and fire its blade.

VI

As dropping flakes of honey-heavy dew
More soft than slumber's, fell the first note's sound
From strings the swift young hand strayed lightlier through
Than leaves through calm air wheeling toward the ground
Stray down the drifting wind when skies are blue
Nor yet the wings of latter winds unbound,
Ere winter loosen all the Æolian crew
With storm unleashed behind them like a hound.
As lightly rose and sank
Beside a green-flowered bank
The clear first notes his burning boyhood found
To sing her sacred praise
Who rode her city's ways
Clothed with bright hair and with high purpose crowned;
A song of soft presageful breath,
Prefiguring all his love and faith in life and death;

VII

Who should love two things only and only praise
More than all else for ever: even the glory
Of goodly beauty in women, whence all days
Take light whereby death's self seems transitory;
And loftier love than loveliest eyes can raise,
Love that wipes off the miry stains and gory
From Time's worn feet, besmirched on bloodred ways,
And lightens with his light the night of story;
Love that lifts up from dust
Life, and makes darkness just,
And purges as with fire of purgatory
The dense disastrous air,
To burn old falsehood bare
And give the wind its ashes heaped and hoary;
Love, that with eyes of ageless youth
Sees on the breast of Freedom borne her nursling Truth.

VIII

For at his birth the sistering stars were one
That flamed upon it as one fiery star;
Freedom, whose light makes pale the mounting sun,
And Song, whose fires are quenched when Freedom's are.
Of all that love not liberty let none
Love her that fills our lips with fire from far
To mix with winds and seas in unison
And sound athwart life's tideless harbour-bar
Out where our songs fly free
Across time's bounded sea,
A boundless flight beyond the dim sun's car,
Till all the spheres of night
Chime concord round their flight
Too loud for blasts of warring change to mar,
From stars that sang for Homer's birth
To these that gave our Landor welcome back from earth

IX

Shine, as above his cradle, on his grave,
Stars of our worship, lights of our desire!
For never man that heard the world's wind rave
To you was truer in trust of heart and lyre:
Nor Greece nor England on a brow more brave
Beheld your flame against the wind burn higher:
Nor all the gusts that blanch life's worldly wave
With surf and surge could quench its flawless fire:
No blast of all that blow
Might bid the torch burn low
That lightens on us yet as o'er his pyre,
Indomitable of storm,
That now no flaws deform
Nor thwart winds baffle ere it all aspire,
One light of godlike breath and flame,
To write on heaven with man's most glorious names his name.

X

The very dawn was dashed with stormy dew
And freaked with fire as when God's hand would mar
Palaces reared of tyrants, and the blue
Deep heaven was kindled round her thunderous car,
That saw how swift a gathering glory grew

About him risen, ere clouds could blind or bar
A splendour strong to burn and burst them through
And mix in one sheer light things near and far.
First flew before his path
Light shafts of love and wrath,
But winged and edged as elder warriors' are;
Then rose a light that showed
Across the midsea road
From radiant Calpe to revealed Masar
The way of war and love and fate
Between the goals of fear and fortune, hope and hate.

XI

Mine own twice banished fathers' harbour-land,
Their nursing-mother France, the well-beloved,
By the arduous blast of sanguine sunrise fanned,
Flamed on him, and his burning lips were moved
As that live statue's throned on Lybian sand
When morning moves it, ere her light faith roved
From promise, and her tyrant's poisonous hand
Fed hope with Corsic honey till she proved
More deadly than despair
And falser even than fair,
Though fairer than all elder hopes removed
As landmarks by the crime
Of inundating time;
Light faith by grief too loud too long reproved:
For even as in some darkling dance
Wronged love changed hands with hate, and turned his heart from France.

XII

But past the snows and summits Pyrenean
Love stronger-winged held more prevailing flight
That o'er Tyrrhene, Iberian, and Ægean
Shores lightened with one storm of sound and light.
From earliest even to hoariest years one pæan
Rang rapture through the fluctuant roar of fight,
From Nestor's tongue in accents Achillean
On death's blind verge dominant over night
For voice as hand and hand
As voice for one fair land
Rose radiant, smote sonorous, past the height
Where darkling pines enrobe
The steel-cold Lake of Gaube,

Deep as dark death and keen as death to smite,
To where on peak or moor or plain
His heart and song and sword were one to strike for Spain.

XIII

Resurgent at his lifted voice and hand
Pale in the light of war or treacherous fate
Song bade before him all their shadows stand
For whom his will unbarred their funeral grate.
The father by whose wrong revenged his land
Was given for sword and fire to desolate
Rose fire-encircled as a burning brand,
Great as the woes he wrought and bore were great.
Fair as she smiled and died,
Death's crowned and breathless bride
Smiled as one living even on craft and hate:
And pity, a star unrisen,
Scarce lit Ferrante's prison
Ere night unnatural closed the natural gate
That gave their life and love and light
To those fair eyes despoiled by fratricide of sight.

XIV

Tears bright and sweet as fire and incense fell
In perfect notes of music-measured pain
On veiled sweet heads that heard not love's farewell
Sob through the song that bade them rise again;
Rise in the light of living song, to dwell
With memories crowned of memory: so the strain
Made soft as heaven the stream that girdles hell
And sweet the darkness of the breathless plain,
And with Elysian flowers
Recrowned the wreathless hours
That mused and mourned upon their works in vain;
For all their works of death
Song filled with light and breath,
And listening grief relaxed her lightening chain;
For sweet as all the wide sweet south
She found the song like honey from the lion's mouth.

XV

High from his throne in heaven Simonides,

Crowned with mild aureole of memorial tears
That the everlasting sun of all time sees
All golden, molten from the forge of years,
Smiled, as the gift was laid upon his knees
Of songs that hang like pearls in mourners' ears,
Mild as the murmuring of Hymettian bees
And honied as their harvest, that endears
The toil of flowery days;
And smiling perfect praise
Hailed his one brother mateless else of peers:
Whom we that hear not him
For length of date grown dim
Hear, and the heart grows glad of grief that hears;
And harshest heights of sorrowing hours,
Like snows of Alpine April, melt from tears to flowers.

XVI

Therefore to him the shadow of death was none,
The darkness was not, nor the temporal tomb:
And multitudinous time for him was one,
Who bade before his equal seat of doom
Rise and stand up for judgment in the sun
The weavers of the world's large-historied loom,
By their own works of light or darkness done
Clothed round with light or girt about with gloom.
In speech of purer gold
Than even they spake of old
He bade the breath of Sidney's lips relume
The fire of thought and love
That made his bright life move
Through fair brief seasons of benignant bloom
To blameless music ever, strong
As death and sweet as death-annihilating song.

XVII

Thought gave his wings the width of time to roam,
Love gave his thought strength equal to release
From bonds of old forgetful years, like foam
Vanished, the fame of memories that decrease;
So strongly faith had fledged for flight from home
The soul's large pinions till her strife should cease:
And through the trumpet of a child of Rome
Rang the pure music of the flutes of Greece.
As though some northern hand

Reft from the Latin land
A spoil more costly than the Colchian fleece
To clothe with golden sound
Of old joy newly found
And rapture as of penetrating peace
The naked north-wind's cloudiest clime,
And give its darkness light of the old Sicilian time.

XVIII

He saw the brand that fired the towers of Troy
Fade, and the darkness at Oenone's prayer
Close upon her that closed upon her boy,
For all the curse of godhead that she bare;
And the Apollonian serpent gleam and toy
With scathless maiden limbs and shuddering hair;
And his love smitten in their dawn of joy
Leave Pan the pine-leaf of her change to wear;
And one in flowery coils
Caught as in fiery toils
Smite Calydon with mourning unaware;
And where her low turf shrine
Showed Modesty divine
The fairest mother's daughter far more fair
Hide on her breast the heavenly shame
That kindled once with love should kindle Troy with flame.

XIX

Nor less the light of story than of song
With graver glories girt his godlike head,
Reverted alway from the temporal throng
Of lives that live not toward the living dead.
The shadows and the splendours of their throng
Made bright and dark about his board and bed
The lines of life and vision, sweet or strong
With sound of lutes or trumpets blown, that led
Forth of the ghostly gate
Opening in spite of fate
Shapes of majestic or tumultuous tread,
Divine and direful things,
These foul as priests or kings,
Those fair as heaven or love or freedom, red
With blood and green with palms and white
With raiment woven of deeds divine and words of light.

The thunder-fire of Cromwell, and the ray
That keeps the place of Phocion's name serene
And clears the cloud from Kosciusko's day,
Alternate as dark hours with bright between,
Met in the heaven of his high thought, which lay
For all stars open that all eyes had seen
Rise on the night or twilight of the way
Where feet of human hopes and fears had been.
Again the sovereign word
On Milton's lips was heard
Living: again the tender three days' queen
Drew bright and gentle breath
On the sharp edge of death:
And, staged again to show of mortal scene,
Tiberius, ere his name grew dire,
Wept, stainless yet of empire, tears of blood and fire.

Most ardent and most awful and most fond,
The fervour of his Apollonian eye
Yearned upon Hellas, yet enthralled in bond
Of time whose years beheld her and past by
Silent and shameful, till she rose and donned
The casque again of Pallas; for her cry
Forth of the past and future, depths beyond
This where the present and its tyrants lie,
As one great voice of twain
For him had pealed again,
Heard but of hearts high as her own was high,
High as her own and his
And pure as love's heart is,
That lives though hope at once and memory die:
And with her breath his clarion's blast
Was filled as cloud with fire or future souls with past.

As a wave only obsequious to the wind
Leaps to the lifting breeze that bids it leap,
Large-hearted, and its thickening mane be thinned
By the strong god's breath moving on the deep
From utmost Atlas even to extremest Ind

That shakes the plain where no men sow nor reap,
So, moved with wrath toward men that ruled and sinned
And pity toward all tears he saw men weep,
Arose to take man's part
His loving lion heart,
Kind as the sun's that has in charge to keep
Earth and the seed thereof
Safe in his lordly love,
Strong as sheer truth and soft as very sleep;
The mightiest heart since Milton's leapt,
The gentlest since the gentlest heart of Shakespeare slept.

XXIII

Like the wind's own on her divided sea
His song arose on Corinth, and aloud
Recalled her Isthmian song and strife when she
Was thronged with glories as with gods in crowd
And as the wind's own spirit her breath was free
And as the heaven's own heart her soul was proud,
But freer and prouder stood no son than he
Of all she bare before her heart was bowed;
None higher than he who heard
Medea's keen last word
Transpierce her traitor, and like a rushing cloud
That sundering shows a star
Saw pass her thunderous car
And a face whiter and deadlier than a shroud
That lightened from it, and the brand
Of tender blood that falling seared his suppliant hand.

XXIV

More fair than all things born and slain of fate,
More glorious than all births of days and nights,
He bade the spirit of man regenerate,
Rekindling, rise and reassume the rights
That in high seasons of his old estate
Clothed him and armed with majesties and mights
Heroic, when the times and hearts were great
And in the depths of ages rose the heights
Radiant of high deeds done
And souls that matched the sun
For splendour with the lightnings of their lights
Whence even their uttered names
Burn like the strong twin flames

Of song that shakes a throne and steel that smites;
As on Thermopylæ when shone
Leonidas, on Syracuse Timoleon.

XXV

Or, sweeter than the breathless buds when spring
With smiles and tears and kisses bids them breathe,
Fell with its music from his quiring string
Fragrance of pine-leaves and odorous heath
Twined round the lute whereto he sighed to sing
Of the oak that screened and showed its maid beneath,
Who seeing her bee crawl back with broken wing
Faded, a fairer flower than all her wreath,
And paler, though her oak
Stood scathless of the stroke
More sharp than edge of axe or wolfish teeth,
That mixed with mortals dead
Her own half heavenly head
And life incorporate with a sylvan sheath,
And left the wild rose and the dove
A secret place and sacred from all guests but Love.

XXVI

But in the sweet clear fields beyond the river
Dividing pain from peace and man from shade
He saw the wings that there no longer quiver
Sink of the hours whose parting footfalls fade
On ears which hear the rustling amaranth shiver
With sweeter sound of wind than ever made
Music on earth: departing, they deliver
The soul that shame or wrath or sorrow swayed;
And round the king of men
Clash the clear arms again,
Clear of all soil and bright as laurel braid,
That rang less high for joy
Through the gates fallen of Troy
Than here to hail the sacrificial maid,
Iphigeneia, when the ford
Fast-flowing of sorrows brought her father and their lord.

XXVII

And in the clear gulf of the hollow sea

He saw light glimmering through the grave green gloom
That hardly gave the sun's eye leave to see
Cymodameia; but nor tower nor tomb,
No tower on earth, no tomb of waves may be,
That may not sometime by diviner doom
Be plain and pervious to the poet; he
Bids time stand back from him and fate make room
For passage of his feet,
Strong as their own are fleet,
And yield the prey no years may reassume
Through all their clamorous track,
Nor night nor day win back
Nor give to darkness what his eyes illume
And his lips bless for ever: he
Knows what earth knows not, sings truth sung not of the sea.

XXVIII

Before the sentence of a curule chair
More sacred than the Roman, rose and stood
To take their several doom the imperial pair
Diversely born of Venus, and in mood
Diverse as their one mother, and as fair,
Though like two stars contrasted, and as good,
Though different as dark eyes from golden hair;
One as that iron planet red like blood
That bears among the stars
Fierce witness of her Mars
In bitter fire by her sweet light subdued;
One, in the gentler skies
Sweet as her amorous eyes:
One proud of worlds and seas and darkness rude
Composed and conquered; one content
With lightnings from loved eyes of lovers lightly sent.

XXIX

And where Alpheus and where Ladon ran
Radiant, by many a rushy and rippling cove
More known to glance of god than wandering man,
He sang the strife of strengths divine that strove,
Unequal, one with other, for a span,
Who should be friends for ever in heaven above
And here on pastoral earth: Arcadian Pan,
And the awless lord of kings and shepherds, Love:
All the sweet strife and strange

With fervid counterchange
Till one fierce wail through many a glade and grove
Rang, and its breath made shiver
The reeds of many a river,
And the warm airs waxed wintry that it clove,
Keen-edged as ice-retempered brand;
Nor might god's hurt find healing save of godlike hand.

XXX

As when the jarring gates of thunder ope
Like earthquake felt in heaven, so dire a cry,
So fearful and so fierce—'Give the sword scope!'—
Rang from a daughter's lips, darkening the sky
To the extreme azure of all its cloudless cope
With starless horror: nor the God's own eye
Whose doom bade smite, whose ordinance bade hope,
Might well endure to see the adulteress die,
The husband-slayer fordone
By swordstroke of her son,
Unutterable, unimaginable on high,
On earth abhorrent, fell
Beyond all scourge of hell,
Yet righteous as redemption: Love stood nigh,
Mute, sister-like, and closer clung
Than all fierce forms of threatening coil and maddening tongue.

XXXI

All these things heard and seen and sung of old,
He heard and saw and sang them. Once again
Might foot of man tread, eye of man behold
Things unbeholden save of ancient men,
Ways save by gods untrodden. In his hold
The staff that stayed through some Ætnean glen
The steps of the most highest, most awful-souled
And mightiest-mouthed of singers, even as then
Became a prophet's rod,
A lyre on fire of God,
Being still the staff of exile: yea, as when
The voice poured forth on us
Was even of Æschylus,
And his one word great as the crying of ten,
Crying in men's ears of wrath toward wrong,
Of love toward right immortal, sanctified with song.

XXXII

Him too whom none save one before him ever
Beheld, nor since hath man again beholden,
Whom Dante seeing him saw not, nor the giver
Of all gifts back to man by time withholden,
Shakespeare—him too, whom sea-like ages sever,
As waves divide men's eyes from lights upholden
To landward, from our songs that find him never,
Seeking, though memory fire and hope embolden—
Him too this one song found,
And raised at its sole sound
Up from the dust of darkling dreams and olden
Legends forlorn of breath,
Up from the deeps of death,
Ulysses: him whose name turns all songs golden,
The wise divine strong soul, whom fate
Could make no less than change and chance beheld him great.

XXXIII

Nor stands the seer who raised him less august
Before us, nor in judgment frail and rathe,
Less constant or less loving or less just,
But fruitful-ripe and full of tender faith,
Holding all high and gentle names in trust
Of time for honour; so his quickening breath
Called from the darkness of their martyred dust
Our sweet Saints Alice and Elizabeth,
Revived and reinspired
With speech from heavenward fired
By love to say what Love the Archangel saith
Only, nor may such word
Save by such ears be heard
As hear the tongues of angels after death
Descending on them like a dove
Has taken all earthly sense of thought away but love.

XXXIV

All sweet, all sacred, all heroic things,
All generous names and loyal, and all wise,
With all his heart in all its wayfarings
He sought, and worshipped, seeing them with his eyes
In very present glory, clothed with wings

Of words and deeds and dreams immortal, rise
Visible more than living slaves and kings,
Audible more than actual vows and lies:
These, with scorn's fieriest rod,
These and the Lord their God,
The Lord their likeness, tyrant of the skies
As they Lord Gods of earth,
These with a rage of mirth
He mocked and scourged and spat on, in such wise
That none might stand before his rod,
And these being slain the Spirit alone be lord or God.

XXXV

For of all souls for all time glorious none
Loved Freedom better, of all who have loved her best,
Than he who wrote that scripture of the sun
Writ as with fire and light on heaven's own crest,
Of all words heard on earth the noblest one
That ever spake for souls and left them blest:
GLADLY WE SHOULD REST EVER, HAD WE WON
FREEDOM: WE HAVE LOST, AND VERY GLADLY REST.
O poet hero, lord
And father, we record
Deep in the burning tablets of the breast
Thankfully those divine
And living words of thine
For faith and comfort in our hearts imprest
With strokes engraven past hurt of years
And lines inured with fire of immemorial tears.

XXXVI

But who being less than thou shall sing of thee
Words worthy of more than pity or less than scorn?
Who sing the golden garland woven of three,
Thy daughters, Graces mightier than the morn,
More godlike than the graven gods men see
Made all but all immortal, human born
And heavenly natured? With the first came He,
Led by the living hand, who left forlorn
Life by his death, and time
More by his life sublime
Than by the lives of all whom all men mourn,
And even for mourning praise
Heaven, as for all those days

These dead men's lives clothed round with glories worn
By memory till all time lie dead,
And higher than all behold the bay round Shakespeare's head.

XXXVII

Then, fairer than the fairest Grace of ours,
Came girt with Grecian gold the second Grace,
And verier daughter of his most perfect hours
Than any of latter time or alien place
Named, or with hair inwoven of English flowers
Only, nor wearing on her statelier face
The lordlier light of Athens. All the Powers
That graced and guarded round that holiest race,
That heavenliest and most high
Time hath seen live and die,
Poured all their power upon him to retrace
The erased immortal roll
Of Love's most sovereign scroll
And Wisdom's warm from Freedom's wide embrace,
The scroll that on Aspasia's knees
Laid once made manifest the Olympian Pericles.

XXXVIII

Clothed on with tenderest weft of Tuscan air,
Came laughing like Etrurian spring the third,
With green Valdelsa's hill-flowers in her hair
Deep-drenched with May-dews, in her voice the bird
Whose voice hath night and morning in it; fair
As the ambient gold of wall-flowers that engird
The walls engirdling with a circling stair
My sweet San Gimignano: nor a word
Fell from her flowerlike mouth
Not sweet with all the south;
As though the dust shrined in Certaldo stirred
And spake, as o'er it shone
That bright Pentameron,
And his own vines again and chestnuts heard
Boccaccio: nor swift Elsa's chime
Mixed not her golden babble with Petrarca's rhyme.

XXXIX

No lovelier laughed the garden which receives

Yet, and yet hides not from our following eyes
With soft rose-laurels and low strawberry-leaves,
Ternissa, sweet as April-coloured skies,
Bowed like a flowering reed when May's wind heaves
The reed-bed that the stream kisses and sighs,
In love that shrinks and murmurs and believes
What yet the wisest of the starriest wise
Whom Greece might ever hear
Speaks in the gentlest ear
That ever heard love's lips philosophize
With such deep-reasoning words
As blossoms use and birds,
Nor heeds Leontion lingering till they rise
Far off, in no wise over far,
Beneath a heaven all amorous of its first-born star.

XL

What sound, what storm and splendour of what fire,
Darkening the light of heaven, lightening the night,
Rings, rages, flashes round what ravening pyre
That makes time's face pale with its reflex light
And leaves on earth, who seeing might scarce respire,
A shadow of red remembrance? Right nor might
Alternating wore ever shapes more dire
Nor manifest in all men's awful sight
In form and face that wore
Heaven's light and likeness more
Than these, or held suspense men's hearts at height
More fearful, since man first
Slaked with man's blood his thirst,
Than when Rome clashed with Hannibal in fight,
Till tower on ruining tower was hurled
Where Scipio stood, and Carthage was not in the world.

XLI

Nor lacked there power of purpose in his hand
Who carved their several praise in words of gold
To bare the brows of conquerors and to brand,
Made shelterless of laurels bought and sold
For price of blood or incense, dust or sand,
Triumph or terror. He that sought of old
His father Ammon in a stranger's land,
And shrank before the serpentining fold,
Stood in our seer's wide eye

No higher than man most high,
And lowest in heart when highest in hope to hold
Fast as a scripture furled
The scroll of all the world
Sealed with his signet: nor the blind and bold
First thief of empire, round whose head
Swarmed carrion flies for bees, on flesh for violets fed.[1]

XLII

As fire that kisses, killing with a kiss,
He saw the light of death, riotous and red,
Flame round the bent brows of Semiramis
Re-risen, and mightier, from the Assyrian dead,
Kindling, as dawn a frost-bound precipice,
The steely snows of Russia, for the tread
Of feet that felt before them crawl and hiss
The snaky lines of blood violently shed.
Like living creeping things
That writhe but have no stings
To scare adulterers from the imperial bed
Bowed with its load of lust,
Or chill the ravenous gusts
That made her body a fire from heel to head;
Or change her high bright spirit and clear,
For all its mortal stains, from taint of fraud or fear.

XLIII

As light that blesses, hallowing with a look;
He saw the godhead in Vittoria's face
Shine soft on Buonarroti's, till he took,
Albeit himself God, a more godlike grace,
A strength more heavenly to confront and brook
All ill things coiled about his worldly race,
From the bright scripture of that present book
Wherein his tired grand eyes got power to trace
Comfort more sweet than youth,
And hope whose child was truth,
And love that brought forth sorrow for a space,
Only that she might bear
Joy: these things, written there,
Made even his soul's high heaven a heavenlier place,
Perused with eyes whose glory and glow
Had in their fires the spirit of Michael Angelo.

With balms and dews of blessing he consoled
The fair fame wounded by the black priest's fang,
Giovanna's, and washed off her blithe and bold
Boy-bridegroom's blood, that seemed so long to hang
On her fair hand, even till the stain of old
Was cleansed with healing song, that after sang
Sharp truth by sweetest singers' lips untold
Of pale Beatrice, though her death-note rang
From other strings divine
Ere his rekindling line
With yet more piteous and intolerant pang
Pierced all men's hearts anew
That heard her passion through
Till fierce from throes of fiery pity sprang
Wrath, armed for chase of monstrous beasts,
Strong to lay waste the kingdom of the seed of priests.

He knew the high-souled humbleness, the mirth
And majesty of meanest men born free,
That made with Luther's or with Hofer's birth
The whole world worthier of the sun to see:
The wealth of spirit among the snows, the dearth
Wherein souls festered by the servile sea
That saw the lowest of even crowned heads on earth
Thronged round with worship in Parthenope.
His hand bade Justice guide
Her child Tyrannicide,
Light winged by fire that brings the dawn to be;
And pierced with Tyrrel's dart
Again the riotous heart
That mocked at mercy's tongue and manhood's knee:
And oped the cell where kinglike death
Hung o'er her brows discrowned who bare Elizabeth.

Toward Spenser or toward Bacon proud or kind
He bared the heart of Essex, twain and one,
For the base heart that soiled the starry mind
Stern, for the father in his child undone
Soft as his own toward children, stamped and signed

With their sweet image visibly set on
As by God's hand, clear as his own designed
The likeness radiant out of ages gone
That none may now destroy
Of that high Roman boy
Whom Julius and Cleopatra saw their son
True-born of sovereign seed,
Foredoomed even thence to bleed,
The stately grace of bright Cæsarion,
The head unbent, the heart unbowed,
That not the shadow of death could make less clear and proud.

XLVII

With gracious gods he communed, honouring thus
At once by service and similitude,
Service devout and worship emulous
Of the same golden Muses once they wooed,
The names and shades adored of all of us,
The nurslings of the brave world's earlier brood,
Grown gods for us themselves: Theocritus
First, and more dear Catullus, names bedewed
With blessings bright like tears
From the old memorial years,
And loves and lovely laughters, every mood
Sweet as the drops that fell
Of their own oenomel
From living lips to cheer the multitude
That feeds on words divine, and grows
More worthy, seeing their world re-blossom like a rose.

XLVIII

Peace, the soft seal of long life's closing story,
The silent music that no strange note jars,
Crowned not with gentler hand the years that glory
Crowned, but could hide not all the spiritual scars
Time writes on the inward strengths of warriors hoary
With much long warfare, and with gradual bars
Blindly pent in: but these, being transitory,
Broke, and the power came back that passion mars:
And at the lovely last
Above all anguish past
Before his own the sightless eyes like stars
Arose that watched arise
Like stars in other skies

Above the strife of ships and hurtling cars
The Dioscurian songs divine
That lighten all the world with lightning of their line.

He sang the last of Homer, having sung
The last of his Ulysses. Bright and wide
For him time's dark strait ways, like clouds that clung
About the day-star, doubtful to divide,
Waxed in his spiritual eyeshot, and his tongue
Spake as his soul bore witness, that descried,
Like those twin towering lights in darkness hung,
Homer, and grey Laertes at his side
Kingly as kings are none
Beneath a later sun,
And the sweet maiden ministering in pride
To sovereign and to sage
In their more sweet old age:
These things he sang, himself as old, and died.
And if death be not, if life be,
As Homer and as Milton are in heaven is he.

Poet whose large-eyed loyalty of love
Was pure toward all high poets, all their kind
And all bright words and all sweet works thereof;
Strong like the sun, and like the sunlight kind;
Heart that no fear but every grief might move
Wherewith men's hearts were bound of powers that bind;
The purest soul that ever proof could prove
From taint of tortuous or of envious mind;
Whose eyes elate and clear
Nor shame nor ever fear
But only pity or glorious wrath could blind;
Name set for love apart,
Held lifelong in my heart,
Face like a father's toward my face inclined;
No gilts like thine are mine to give,
Who by thine own words only bid thee hail, and live.

[1] Thy lifelong works, Napoleon, who shall write?
Time, in his children's blood who takes delight.
From the Greek of Landor.

GRAND CHORUS OF BIRDS

FROM ARISTOPHANES

Attempted in English verse after the original metre.

I was allured into the audacity of this experiment by consideration of a fact which hitherto does not seem to have been taken into consideration by any translator of the half divine humourist in whose incomparable genius the highest qualities of Rabelais were fused and harmonized with the supremest gifts of Shelley: namely, that his marvellous metrical invention of the anapæstic heptameter was almost exactly reproducible in a language to which all variations and combinations of anapæstic, iambic, or trochaic metre are as natural and pliable as all dactylic and spondaic forms of verse are unnatural and abhorrent. As it happens, this highest central interlude of a most adorable masterpiece is as easy to detach from its dramatic setting, and even from its lyrical context, as it was easy to give line for line of it in English. In two metrical points only does my version vary from the verbal pattern of the original. I have of course added rhymes, and double rhymes, as necessary makeweights for the imperfection of an otherwise inadequate language; and equally of course I have not attempted the impossible and undesirable task of reproducing the rare exceptional effect of a line overcharged on purpose with a preponderance of heavy-footed spondees: and this for the obvious reason that even if such a line—which I doubt—could be exactly represented, foot by foot and pause for pause, in English, this English line would no more be a verse in any proper sense of the word than is the line I am writing at this moment. And my main intention, or at least my main desire, in the undertaking of this brief adventure, was to renew as far as possible for English ears the music of this resonant and triumphant metre, which goes ringing at full gallop as of horses who

—'dance as 'twere to the music
Their own hoofs make.'

I would not seem over curious in search of an apt or inapt quotation: but nothing can be fitter than a verse of Shakespeare's to praise at once and to describe the most typical verse of Aristophanes.

THE BIRDS. (685-723.)

Come on then, ye dwellers by nature in darkness, and like to the leaves' generations,
That are little of might, that are moulded of mire, unenduring and shadowlike nations,
Poor plumeless ephemerals, comfortless mortals, as visions of creatures fast fleeing,
Lift up your mind unto us that are deathless, and dateless the date of our being:
Us, children of heaven, us, ageless for aye, us, all of whose thoughts are eternal;
That ye may from henceforth, having heard of us all things aright as to matters supernal,
Of the being of birds and beginning of gods, and of streams, and the dark beyond reaching,
Truthfully knowing aright, in my name bid Prodicus pack with his preaching.

It was Chaos and Night at the first, and the blackness of darkness, and hell's broad border,

Earth was not, nor air, neither heaven; when in depths of the womb of the dark without order
First thing first-born of the black-plumed Night was a wind-egg hatched in her bosom,
Whence timely with seasons revolving again sweet Love burst out as a blossom,
Gold wings glittering forth of his back, like whirlwinds gustily turning.
He, after his wedlock with Chaos, whose wings are of darkness, in hell broad-burning,
For his nestlings begat him the race of us first, and upraised us to light new-lighted.
And before this was not the race of the gods, until all things by Love were united;
And of kind united with kind in communion of nature the sky and the sea are
Brought forth, and the earth, and the race of the gods everlasting and blest. So that we are
Far away the most ancient of all things blest. And that we are of Love's generation
There are manifest manifold signs. We have wings, and with us have the Loves habitation;
And manifold fair young folk that forswore love once, ere the bloom of them ended,
Have the men that pursued and desired them subdued, by the help of us only befriended,
With such baits as a quail, a flamingo, a goose, or a cock's comb staring and splendid.

All best good things that befall men come from us birds, as is plain to all reason:
For first we proclaim and make known to them spring, and the winter and autumn in season;
Bid sow, when the crane starts clanging for Afric, in shrill-voiced emigrant number,
And calls to the pilot to hang up his rudder again for the season, and slumber;
And then weave a cloak for Orestes the thief, lest he strip men of theirs if it freezes.
And again thereafter the kite reappearing announces a change in the breezes,
And that here is the season for shearing your sheep of their spring wool.
Then does the swallow
Give you notice to sell your greatcoat, and provide something light for the heat that's to follow.
Thus are we as Ammon or Delphi unto you, Dodona, nay, Phoebus Apollo.
For, as first ye come all to get auguries of birds, even such is in all things your carriage,
Be the matter a matter of trade, or of earning your bread, or of any one's marriage.
And all things ye lay to the charge of a bird that belong to discerning prediction:
Winged fame is a bird, as you reckon: you sneeze, and the sign's as a bird for conviction:
All tokens are 'birds' with you—sounds too, and lackeys, and donkeys.
Then must it not follow
That we ARE to you all as the manifest godhead that speaks in prophetic Apollo?

October 19, 1880.

OFF SHORE

When the might of the summer
Is most on the sea;
When the days overcome her
With joy but to be,
With rapture of royal enchantment, and sorcery that sets her not free,

But for hours upon hours
As a thrall she remains
Spell-bound as with flowers

And content in their chains,
And her loud steeds fret not, and lift not a lock of their deep white manes;

Then only, far under
In the depths of her hold,
Some gleam of its wonder
Man's eye may behold,
Its wild-weed forests of crimson and russet and olive and gold.

Still deeper and dimmer
And goodlier they glow
For the eyes of the swimmer
Who scans them below
As he crosses the zone of their flowerage that knows not of sunshine and snow.

Soft blossomless frondage
And foliage that gleams
As to prisoners in bondage
The light of their dreams,
The desire of a dawn unbeholden, with hope on the wings of its beams.

Not as prisoners entombed
Waxen haggard and wizen,
But consoled and illumed
In the depths of their prison
With delight of the light everlasting and vision of dawn on them risen,

From the banks and the beds
Of the waters divine
They lift up their heads
And the flowers of them shine
Through the splendour of darkness that clothes them of water that glimmers like wine.

Bright bank over bank
Making glorious the gloom,
Soft rank upon rank,
Strange bloom after bloom,
They kindle the liquid low twilight, the dusk of the dim sea's womb.

Through the subtle and tangible
Gloom without form,
Their branches, infrangible
Ever of storm
Spread softer their sprays than the shoots of the woodland when April is warm.

As the flight of the thunder, full
Charged with its word,
Dividing the wonderful

Depths like a bird,
Speaks wrath and delight to the heart of the night that exults to have heard,

So swiftly, though soundless
In silence's ear,
Light, winged from the boundless
Blue depths full of cheer,
Speaks joy to the heart of the waters that part not before him, but hear.

Light, perfect and visible
Godhead of God,
God indivisible,
Lifts but his rod,
And the shadows are scattered in sunder, and darkness is light at his nod.

At the touch of his wand,
At the nod of his head
From the spaces beyond
Where the dawn hath her bed,
Earth, water, and air are transfigured, and rise as one risen from the dead.

He puts forth his hand,
And the mountains are thrilled
To the heart as they stand
In his presence, fulfilled
With his glory that utters his grace upon earth, and her sorrows are stilled.

The moan of her travail
That groans for the light
Till dayspring unravel
The weft of the night,
At the sound of the strings of the music of morning, falls dumb with delight.

He gives forth his word,
And the word that he saith,
Ere well it be heard,
Strikes darkness to death;
For the thought of his heart is the sunrise, and dawn as the sound of his breath.

And the strength of its pulses
That passion makes proud
Confounds and convulses
The depths of the cloud
Of the darkness that heaven was engirt with, divided and rent as a shroud,

As the veil of the shrine
Of the temple of old
When darkness divine

Over noonday was rolled;
So the heart of the night by the pulse of the light is convulsed and controlled.

And the sea's heart, groaning
For glories withdrawn,
And the waves' mouths, moaning
All night for the dawn,
Are uplift as the hearts and the mouths of the singers on leaside and lawn.

And the sound of the quiring
Of all these as one,
Desired and desiring
Till dawn's will be done,
Fills full with delight of them heaven till it burns as the heart of the sun.

Till the waves too inherit
And waters take part
In the sense of the spirit
That breathes from his heart,
And are kindled with music as fire when the lips of the morning part,

With music unheard
In the light of her lips,
In the life-giving word
Of the dewfall that drips
On the grasses of earth, and the wind that enkindles the wings of the ships.

White glories of wings
As of seafaring birds
That flock from the springs
Of the sunrise in herds
With the wind for a herdsman, and hasten or halt at the change of his words.

As the watchword's change
When the wind's note shifts,
And the skies grow strange,
And the white squall drifts
Up sharp from the sea-line, vexing the sea till the low cloud lifts.

At the charge of his word
Bidding pause, bidding haste,
When the ranks are stirred
And the lines displaced,
They scatter as wild swans parting adrift on the wan green waste.

At the hush of his word
In a pause of his breath
When the waters have heard

His will that he saith,
They stand as a flock penned close in its fold for division of death.

As a flock by division
Of death to be thinned,
As the shades in a vision
Of spirits that sinned;
So glimmer their shrouds and their sheetings as clouds on the stream of the wind.

But the sun stands fast,
And the sea burns bright,
And the flight of them past
Is no more than the flight
Of the snow-soft swarm of serene wings poised and afloat in the light.

Like flowers upon flowers
In a festival way
When hours after hours
Shed grace on the day,
White blossom-like butterflies hover and gleam through the snows of the spray.

Like snow-coloured petals
Of blossoms that flee
From storm that unsettles
The flower as the tree
They flutter, a legion of flowers on the wing, through the field of the sea.

Through the furrowless field
Where the foam-blossoms blow
And the secrets are sealed
Of their harvest below
They float in the path of the sunbeams, as flakes or as blossoms of snow.

Till the sea's ways darken,
And the God, withdrawn,
Give ear not or hearken
If prayer on him fawn,
And the sun's self seem but a shadow, the noon as a ghost of the dawn.

No shadow, but rather
God, father of song,
Shew grace to me, Father
God, loved of me long,
That I lose not the light of thy face, that my trust in thee work me not wrong.

While yet I make forward
With face toward thee
Not turned yet in shoreward,

Be thine upon me;
Be thy light on my forehead or ever I turn it again from the sea.

As a kiss on my brow
Be the light of thy grace,
Be thy glance on me now
From the pride of thy place:
As the sign of a sire to a son be the light on my face of thy face.

Thou wast father of olden
Times hailed and adored,
And the sense of thy golden
Great harp's monochord
Was the joy in the soul of the singers that hailed thee for master and lord.

Fair father of all
In thy ways that have trod,
That have risen at thy call,
That have thrilled at thy nod,
Arise, shine, lighten upon me, O sun that we see to be God.

As my soul has been dutiful
Only to thee,
O God most beautiful,
Lighten thou me,
As I swim through the dim long rollers, with eyelids uplift from the sea.

Be praised and adored of us
All in accord,
Father and lord of us
Alway adored,
The slayer and the stayer and the harper, the light of us all and our lord.

At the sound of thy lyre,
At the touch of thy rod,
Air quickens to fire
By the foot of thee trod,
The saviour and healer and singer, the living and visible God.

The years are before thee
As shadows of thee,
As men that adore thee,
As cloudlets that flee:
But thou art the God, and thy kingdom is heaven, and thy shrine is the sea.

AFTER NINE YEARS

Primâ dicte mihi, summâ dicende Camenâ.

I

The shadows fallen of years are nine
Since heaven grew seven times more divine
With thy soul entering, and the dearth
Of souls on earth
Grew sevenfold sadder, wanting One
Whose light of life, quenched here and done,
Burns there eternal as the sun.

II

Beyond all word, beyond all deed,
Beyond all thought beloved, what need
Has death or love that speech should be,
Hast thou of me?
I had no word, no prayer, no cry,
To praise or hail or mourn thee by,
As when thou too wast man as I.

III

Nay, never, nor as any born
Save one whose name priests turn to scorn,
Who haply, though we know not now,
Was man as thou,
A wanderer branded with men's blame,
Loved past man's utterance: yea, the same,
Perchance, and as his name thy name.

IV

Thou wast as very Christ—not he
Degraded into Deity,
And priest-polluted by such prayer
As poisons air,
Tongue-worship of the tongue that slays,
False faith and parricidal praise:
But the man crowned with suffering days.

God only, being of all mankind
Most manlike, of most equal mind
And heart most perfect, more than can
Be heart of man
Once in ten ages, born to be
As haply Christ was, and as we
Knew surely, seeing, and worshipped thee.

To know thee—this at least was ours,
God, clothed upon with human hours,
O face beloved, O spirit adored,
Saviour and lord!
That wast not only for thine own
Redeemer—not of these alone
But all to whom thy word was known.

Ten years have wrought their will with me
Since last my words took wing for thee
Who then wast even as now above
Me, and my love.
As then thou knewest not scorn, so now
With that beloved benignant brow
Take these of him whose light wast thou.

FOR A PORTRAIT OF FELICE ORSINI

Steadfast as sorrow, fiery sad, and sweet
With underthoughts of love and faith, more strong
Than doubt and hate and all ill thoughts which throng,
Haply, round hope's or fear's world-wandering feet
That find no rest from wandering till they meet
Death, bearing palms in hand and crowns of song;
His face, who thought to vanquish wrong with wrong,
Erring, and make rage and redemption meet,
Havoc and freedom; weaving in one weft
Good with his right hand, evil with his left;
But all a hero lived and erred and died;

Looked thus upon the living world he left
So bravely that with pity less than pride
Men hail him Patriot and Tyrannicide.

EVENING ON THE BROADS

Over two shadowless waters, adrift as a pinnace in peril,
Hangs as in heavy suspense, charged with irresolute light,
Softly the soul of the sunset upholden awhile on the sterile
Waves and wastes of the land, half repossessed by the night.
Inland glimmer the shallows asleep and afar in the breathless
Twilight: yonder the depths darken afar and asleep.
Slowly the semblance of death out of heaven descends on the deathless
Waters: hardly the light lives on the face of the deep—
Hardly, but here for awhile. All over the grey soft shallow
Hover the colours and clouds of the twilight, void of a star.
As a bird unfledged is the broad-winged night, whose winglets are callow
Yet, but soon with their plumes will she cover her brood from afar,
Cover the brood of her worlds that cumber the skies with their blossom
Thick as the darkness of leaf-shadowed spring is encumbered with flowers.
World upon world is enwound in the bountiful girth of her bosom,
Warm and lustrous with life lovely to look on as ours.
Still is the sunset adrift as a spirit in doubt that dissembles
Still with itself, being sick of division and dimmed by dismay—
Nay, not so; but with love and delight beyond passion it trembles,
Fearful and fain of the night, lovely with love of the day:
Fain and fearful of rest that is like unto death, and begotten
Out of the womb of the tomb, born of the seed of the grave:
Lovely with shadows of loves that are only not wholly forgotten,
Only not wholly suppressed by the dark as a wreck by the wave.
Still there linger the loves of the morning and noon, in a vision
Blindly beheld, but in vain: ghosts that are tired, and would rest.
But the glories beloved of the night rise all too dense for division,
Deep in the depth of her breast sheltered as doves in a nest.
Fainter the beams of the loves of the daylight season enkindled
Wane, and the memories of hours that were fair with the love of them fade:
Loftier, aloft of the lights of the sunset stricken and dwindled,
Gather the signs of the love at the heart of the night new-made.
New-made night, new-born of the sunset, immeasurable, endless,
Opens the secret of love hid from of old in her heart,
In the deep sweet heart full-charged with faultless love of the friendless
Spirits of men that are eased when the wheels of the sun depart.
Still is the sunset afloat as a ship on the waters upholden
Full-sailed, wide-winged, poised softly for ever asway—
Nay, not so, but at least for a little, awhile at the golden
Limit of arching air fain for an hour to delay.

Here on the bar of the sand-bank, steep yet aslope to the gleaming
Waste of the water without, waste of the water within,
Lights overhead and lights underneath seem doubtfully dreaming
Whether the day be done, whether the night may begin.
Far and afar and farther again they falter and hover,
Warm on the water and deep in the sky and pale on the cloud:
Colder again and slowly remoter, afraid to recover
Breath, yet fain to revive, as it seems, from the skirt of the shroud.
Faintly the heartbeats shorten and pause of the light in the westward
Heaven, as eastward quicken the paces of star upon star
Hurried and eager of life as a child that strains to the breast-ward
Eagerly, yearning forth of the deeps where the ways of them are,
Glad of the glory of the gift of their life and the wealth of its wonder,
Fain of the night and the sea and the sweet wan face of the earth.
Over them air grows deeper, intense with delight in them: under
Things are thrilled in their sleep as with sense of a sure new birth.
But here by the sand-bank watching, with eyes on the sea-line, stranger
Grows to me also the weight of the sea-ridge gazed on of me,
Heavily heaped up, changefully changeless, void though of danger
Void not of menace, but full of the might of the dense dull sea.
Like as the wave is before me, behind is the bank deep-drifted;
Yellow and thick as the bank is behind me in front is the wave.
As the wall of a prison imprisoning the mere is the girth of it lifted:
But the rampire of water in front is erect as the wall of a grave.
And the crests of it crumble and topple and change, but the wall is not broken:
Standing still dry-shod, I see it as higher than my head,
Moving inland alway again, reared up as in token
Still of impending wrath still in the foam of it shed.
And even in the pauses between them, dividing the rollers in sunder,
High overhead seems ever the sea-line fixed as a mark,
And the shore where I stand as a valley beholden of hills whence thunder
Cloud and torrent and storm, darkening the depths of the dark.
Up to the sea, not upon it or over it, upward from under
Seems he to gaze, whose eyes yearn after it here from the shore:
A wall of turbid water, aslope to the wide sky's wonder
Of colour and cloud, it climbs, or spreads as a slanted floor.
And the large lights change on the face of the mere like things that were living,
Winged and wonderful, beams like as birds are that pass and are free:
But the light is dense as darkness, a gift withheld in the giving,
That lies as dead on the fierce dull face of the landward sea.
Stained and stifled and soiled, made earthier than earth is and duller,
Grimly she puts back light as rejected, a thing put away:
No transparent rapture, a molten music of colour;
No translucent love taken and given of the day.
Fettered and marred and begrimed is the light's live self on her falling,
As the light of a man's life lighted the fume of a dungeon mars:
Only she knows of the wind, when her wrath gives ear to him calling;
The delight of the light she knows not, nor answers the sun or the stars.

Love she hath none to return for the luminous love of their giving:
None to reflect from the bitter and shallow response of her heart
Yearly she feeds on her dead, yet herself seems dead and not living,
Or confused as a soul heavy-laden with trouble that will not depart.
In the sound of her speech to the darkness the moan of her evil remorse is,
Haply, for strong ships gnawed by the dog-toothed sea-bank's fang
And trampled to death by the rage of the feet of her foam-lipped horses
Whose manes are yellow as plague, and as ensigns of pestilence hang,
That wave in the foul faint air of the breath of a death-stricken city;
So menacing heaves she the manes of her rollers knotted with sand,
Discoloured, opaque, suspended in sign as of strength without pity,
That shake with flameless thunder the low long length of the strand.
Here, far off in the farther extreme of the shore as it lengthens
Northward, lonely for miles, ere ever a village begin,
On the lapsing land that recedes as the growth of the strong sea strengthens
Shoreward, thrusting further and further its outworks in,
Here in Shakespeare's vision, a flower of her kin forsaken,
Lay in her golden raiment alone on the wild wave's edge,
Surely by no shore else, but here on the bank storm-shaken,
Perdita, bright as a dew-drop engilt of the sun on the sedge.
Here on a shore unbeheld of his eyes in a dream he beheld her
Outcast, fair as a fairy, the child of a far-off king:
And over the babe-flower gently the head of a pastoral elder
Bowed, compassionate, hoar as the hawthorn-blossom in spring,
And kind as harvest in autumn: a shelter of shade on the lonely
Shelterless unknown shore scourged of implacable waves:
Here, where the wind walks royal, alone in his kingdom, and only
Sounds to the sedges a wail as of triumph that conquers and craves.
All these waters and wastes are his empire of old, and awaken
From barren and stagnant slumber at only the sound of his breath:
Yet the hunger is eased not that aches in his heart, nor the goal overtaken
That his wide wings yearn for and labour as hearts that yearn after death.
All the solitude sighs and expects with a blind expectation
Somewhat unknown of its own sad heart, grown heart-sick of strife:
Till sometime its wild heart maddens, and moans, and the vast ululation
Takes wing with the clouds on the waters, and wails to be quit of its life.
For the spirit and soul of the waste is the wind, and his wings with their waving
Darken and lighten the darkness and light of it thickened or thinned;
But the heart that impels them is even as a conqueror's insatiably craving
That victory can fill not, as power cannot satiate the want of the wind.
All these moorlands and marshes are full of his might, and oppose not
Aught of defence nor of barrier, of forest or precipice piled:
But the will of the wind works ever as his that desires what he knows not,
And the wail of his want unfulfilled is as one making moan for her child.
And the cry of his triumph is even as the crying of hunger that maddens
The heart of a strong man aching in vain as the wind's heart aches
And the sadness itself of the land for its infinite solitude saddens
More for the sound than the silence athirst for the sound that slakes.

And the sunset at last and the twilight are dead: and the darkness is breathless
With fear of the wind's breath rising that seems and seems not to sleep:
But a sense of the sound of it alway, a spirit unsleeping and deathless,
Ghost or God, evermore moves on the face of the deep.

THE EMPEROR'S PROGRESS

A STUDY IN THREE STAGES

(On the Busts of Nero in the Uffizj.)

I

A child of brighter than the morning's birth
And lovelier than all smiles that may be smiled
Save only of little children undefiled,
Sweet, perfect, witless of their own dear worth,
Live rose of love, mute melody of mirth,
Glad as a bird is when the woods are mild,
Adorable as is nothing save a child,
Hails with wide eyes and lips his life on earth,
His lovely life with all its heaven to be.
And whoso reads the name inscribed or hears
Feels his own heart a frozen well of tears,
Child, for deep dread and fearful pity of thee
Whom God would not let rather die than see
The incumbent horror of impending years.

II

Man, that wast godlike being a child, and now,
No less than kinglike, art no more in sooth
For all thy grace and lordliness of youth,
The crown that bids men's branded foreheads bow
Much more has branded and bowed down thy brow
And gnawn upon it as with fire or tooth
Of steel or snake so sorely, that the truth
Seems here to bear false witness. Is it thou,
Child? and is all the summer of all thy spring
This? are the smiles that drew men's kisses down
All faded and transfigured to the frown
That grieves thy face? Art thou this weary thing?
Then is no slave's load heavier than a crown
And such a thrall no bondman as a king.

III

Misery, beyond all men's most miserable,
Absolute, whole, defiant of defence,
Inevitable, inexplacable, intense,
More vast than heaven is high, more deep than hell,
Past cure or charm of solace or of spell,
Possesses and pervades the spirit and sense
Whereto the expanse of the earth pays tribute; whence
Breeds evil only, and broods on fumes that swell
Rank from the blood of brother and mother and wife.
'Misery of miseries, all is misery,' saith
The heavy fair-faced hateful head, at strife
With its own lusts that burn with feverous breath
Lips which the loathsome bitterness of life
Leaves fearful of the bitterness of death.

THE RESURRECTION OF ALCILIA

(Gratefully inscribed to Dr. A.B. Grosart.)

Sweet song-flower of the Mayspring of our song,
Be welcome to us, with loving thanks and praise
To his good hand who travelling on strange ways
Found thee forlorn and fragrant, lain along
Beneath dead leaves that many a winter's wrong
Had rained and heaped through nigh three centuries' maze
Above thy Maybloom, hiding from our gaze
The life that in thy leaves lay sweet and strong.
For thine have life, while many above thine head
Piled by the wind lie blossomless and dead.
So now disburdened of such load above
That lay as death's own dust upon thee shed
By days too deaf to hear thee like a dove
Murmuring, we hear thee, bird and flower of love.

THE FOURTEENTH OF JULY

(On the refusal by the French Senate of the plenary amnesty demanded by Victor Hugo, in his speech of July 3rd, for the surviving exiles of the Commune.)

Thou shouldst have risen as never dawn yet rose,
Day of the sunrise of the soul of France,

Dawn of the whole world's morning, when the trance
Of all the world had end, and all its woes
Respite, prophetic of their perfect close.
Light of all tribes of men, all names and clans,
Dawn of the whole world's morning and of man's
Flower of the heart of morning's mystic rose,
Dawn of the very dawn of very day,
When the sun brighter breaks night's ruinous prison,
Thou shouldst have risen as yet no dawn has risen,
Evoked of him whose word puts night away,
Our father, at the music of whose word
Exile had ended, and the world had heard.

July 5, 1880.

LAUNCH OF THE LIVADIA

Malâ soluta navis exit alite.
HOR.

Rigged with curses dark.
MILTON.

THE LAUNCH OF THE LIVADIA

I

Gold, and fair marbles, and again more gold,
And space of halls afloat that glance and gleam
Like the green heights of sunset heaven, or seem
The golden steeps of sunrise red and cold
On deserts where dark exile keeps the fold
Fast of the flocks of torment, where no beam
Falls of kind light or comfort save in dream,
These we far off behold not, who behold
The cordage woven of curses, and the decks
With mortal hate and mortal peril paven;
From stem to stern the lines of doom engraven
That mark for sure inevitable wrecks
Those sails predestinate, though no storm vex,
To miss on earth and find in hell their haven.

II

All curses be about her, and all ill
Go with her; heaven be dark above her way,
The gulf beneath her glad and sure of prey,
And, wheresoe'er her prow be pointed, still
The winds of heaven have all one evil will
Conspirant even as hearts of kings to slay
With mouths of kings to lie and smile and pray,
And chiefliest his whose wintrier breath makes chill
With more than winter's and more poisonous cold
The horror of his kingdom toward the north,
The deserts of his kingdom toward the east.
And though death hide not in her direful hold
Be all stars adverse toward her that come forth
Nightly, by day all hours till all have ceased:

III

Till all have ceased for ever, and the sum
Be summed of all the sumless curses told
Out on his head by all dark seasons rolled
Over its cursed and crowned existence, dumb
And blind and stark as though the snows made numb
All sense within it, and all conscience cold,
That hangs round hearts of less imperial mould
Like a snake feeding till their doomsday come.
O heart fast bound of frozen poison, be
All nature's as all true men's hearts to thee,
A two-edged sword of judgment; hope be far
And fear at hand for pilot oversea
With death for compass and despair for star,
And the white foam a shroud for the White Czar.

September 30, 1880.

SIX YEARS OLD

To H.W.M.

Between the springs of six and seven,
Two fresh years' fountains, clear
Of all but golden sand for leaven,
Child, midway passing here,
As earth for love's sake dares bless heaven,
So dare I bless you, dear.

Between two bright well-heads, that brighten
With every breath that blows
Too loud to lull, too low to frighten,
But fain to rock, the rose,
Your feet stand fast, your lit smiles lighten,
That might rear flowers from snows.

You came when winds unleashed were snarling
Behind the frost-bound hours,
A snow-bird sturdier than the starling,
A storm-bird fledged for showers,
That spring might smile to find you, darling,
First born of all the flowers.

Could love make worthy things of worthless,
My song were worth an ear:
Its note should make the days most mirthless
The merriest of the year,
And wake to birth all buds yet birthless
To keep your birthday, dear.

But where your birthday brightens heaven
No need has earth, God knows,
Of light or warmth to melt or leaven
The frost or fog that glows
With sevenfold heavenly lights of seven
Sweet springs that cleave the snows.

Could love make worthy music of you,
And match my Master's powers,
Had even my love less heart to love you,
A better song were ours;
With all the rhymes like stars above you,
And all the words like flowers.

September 30, 1880.

A PARTING SONG

(To a friend leaving England for a year's residence in Australia.)

These winds and suns of spring
That warm with breath and wing
The trembling sleep of earth, till half awake
She laughs and blushes ere her slumber break,

For all good gifts they bring
Require one better thing,
For all the loans of joy they lend us, borrow
One sharper dole of sorrow,
To sunder soon by half a world of sea
Her son from England and my friend from me.

Nor hope nor love nor fear
May speed or stay one year,
Nor song nor prayer may bid, as mine would fain,
The seasons perish and be born again,
Restoring all we lend,
Reluctant, of a friend,
The voice, the hand, the presence and the sight
That lend their life and light
To present gladness and heart-strengthening cheer,
Now lent again for one reluctant year.

So much we lend indeed,
Perforce, by force of need,
So much we must; even these things and no more
The far sea sundering and the sundered shore
A world apart from ours,
So much the imperious hours,
Exact, and spare not; but no more than these
All earth and all her seas
From thought and faith of trust and truth can borrow,
Not memory from desire, nor hope from sorrow.

Through bright and dark and bright
Returns of day and night
I bid the swift year speed and change and give
His breath of life to make the next year live
With sunnier suns for us
A life more prosperous,
And laugh with flowers more fragrant, that shall see
A merrier March for me,
A rosier-girdled race of night with day,
A goodlier April and a tenderer May.

For him the inverted year
Shall mark our seasons here
With alien alternation, and revive
This withered winter, slaying the spring alive
With darts more sharply drawn
As nearer draws the dawn
In heaven transfigured over earth transformed
And with our winters warmed

And wasted with our summers, till the beams
Rise on his face that rose on Dante's dreams.

Till fourfold morning rise
Of starshine on his eyes,
Dawn of the spheres that brand steep heaven across
At height of night with semblance of a cross
Whose grace and ghostly glory
Poured heaven on purgatory
Seeing with their flamelets risen all heaven grow glad
For love thereof it had
And lovely joy of loving; so may these
Make bright with welcome now their southern seas.

O happy stars, whose mirth
The saddest soul on earth
That ever soared and sang found strong to bless,
Lightening his life's harsh load of heaviness
With comfort sown like seed
In dream though not in deed
On sprinkled wastes of darkling thought divine,
Let all your lights now shine
With all as glorious gladness on his eyes
For whom indeed and not in dream they rise.

As those great twins of air
Hailed once with oldworld prayer
Of all folk alway faring forth by sea,
So now may these for grace and guidance be,
To guard his sail and bring
Again to brighten spring
The face we look for and the hand we lack
Still, till they light him back,
As welcome as to first discovering eyes
Their light rose ever, soon on his to rise.

As parting now he goes
From snow-time back to snows,
So back to spring from summer may next year
Restore him, and our hearts receive him here,
The best good gift that spring
Had ever grace to bring
At fortune's happiest hour of star-blest birth
Back to love's homebright earth,
To eyes with eyes that commune, hand with hand,
And the old warm bosom of all our mother-land.

Earth and sea-wind and sea

And stars and sunlight be
Alike all prosperous for him, and all hours
Have all one heart, and all that heart as ours.
All things as good as strange
Crown all the seasons' change
With changing flower and compensating fruit
From one year's ripening root;
Till next year bring us, roused at spring's recall,
A heartier flower and goodlier fruit than all.

March 26, 1880.

TO WALTER THEODORE WATTS

'We are what suns and winds and waters make us.'—LANDOR.

Sea, wind, and sun, with light and sound and breath
The spirit of man fulfilling—these create
That joy wherewith man's life grown passionate
Gains heart to hear and sense to read and faith
To know the secret word our Mother saith
In silence, and to see, though doubt wax great,
Death as the shadow cast by life on fate,
Passing, whose shade we call the shadow of death.

Brother, to whom our Mother as to me
Is dearer than all dreams of days undone,
This song I give you of the sovereign three
That are as life and sleep and death are, one:
A song the sea-wind gave me from the sea,
Where nought of man's endures before the sun.

BY THE NORTH SEA

I.

1.

A land that is lonelier than ruin;
A sea that is stranger than death:
Far fields that a rose never blew in,

Wan waste where the winds lack breath;
Waste endless and boundless and flowerless
But of marsh-blossoms fruitless as free:
Where earth lies exhausted, as powerless
To strive with the sea.

2.

Far flickers the flight of the swallows,
Far flutters the weft of the grass
Spun dense over desolate hollows
More pale than the clouds as they pass:
Thick woven as the weft of a witch is
Round the heart of a thrall that hath sinned,
Whose youth and the wrecks of its riches
Are waifs on the wind.

3.

The pastures are herdless and sheepless,
No pasture or shelter for herds:
The wind is relentless and sleepless,
And restless and songless the birds;
Their cries from afar fall breathless,
Their wings are as lightnings that flee;
For the land has two lords that are deathless:
Death's self, and the sea.

4.

These twain, as a king with his fellow,
Hold converse of desolate speech:
And her waters are haggard and yellow
And crass with the scurf of the beach:
And his garments are grey as the hoary
Wan sky where the day lies dim;
And his power is to her, and his glory,
As hers unto him.

5.

In the pride of his power she rejoices,
In her glory he glows and is glad:
In her darkness the sound of his voice is,
With his breath she dilates and is mad:
'If thou slay me, O death, and outlive me,
Yet thy love hath fulfilled me of thee.'
'Shall I give thee not back if thou give me,

O sister, O sea?'

6.

And year upon year dawns living,
And age upon age drops dead:
And his hand is not weary of giving,
And the thirst of her heart is not fed:
And the hunger that moans in her passion,
And the rage in her hunger that roars,
As a wolf's that the winter lays lash on,
Still calls and implores.

7.

Her walls have no granite for girder,
No fortalice fronting her stands:
But reefs the bloodguiltiest of murder
Are less than the banks of her sands:
These number their slain by the thousand;
For the ship hath no surety to be,
When the bank is abreast of her bows and
Aflush with the sea.

8.

No surety to stand, and no shelter
To dawn out of darkness but one,
Out of waters that hurtle and welter
No succour to dawn with the sun
But a rest from the wind as it passes,
Where, hardly redeemed from the waves,
Lie thick as the blades of the grasses
The dead in their graves.

9.

A multitude noteless of numbers,
As wild weeds cast on an heap:
And sounder than sleep are their slumbers,
And softer than song is their sleep;
And sweeter than all things and stranger
The sense, if perchance it may be,
That the wind is divested of danger
And scatheless the sea.

10.

That the roar of the banks they breasted
Is hurtless as bellowing of herds,
And the strength of his wings that invested
The wind, as the strength of a bird's;
As the sea-mew's might or the swallow's
That cry to him back if he cries,
As over the graves and their hollows
Days darken and rise.

11.

As the souls of the dead men disburdened
And clean of the sins that they sinned,
With a lovelier than man's life guerdoned
And delight as a wave's in the wind,
And delight as the wind's in the billow,
Birds pass, and deride with their glee
The flesh that has dust for its pillow
As wrecks have the sea.

12.

When the ways of the sun wax dimmer,
Wings flash through the dusk like beams;
As the clouds in the lit sky glimmer,
The bird in the graveyard gleams;
As the cloud at its wing's edge whitens
When the clarions of sunrise are heard,
The graves that the bird's note brightens
Grow bright for the bird.

13.

As the waves of the numberless waters
That the wind cannot number who guides
Are the sons of the shore and the daughters
Here lulled by the chime of the tides:
And here in the press of them standing
We know not if these or if we
Live truliest, or anchored to landing
Or drifted to sea.

14.

In the valley he named of decision
No denser were multitudes met
When the soul of the seer in her vision
Saw nations for doom of them set;

Saw darkness in dawn, and the splendour
Of judgment, the sword and the rod;
But the doom here of death is more tender
And gentler the god.

15.

And gentler the wind from the dreary
Sea-banks by the waves overlapped,
Being weary, speaks peace to the weary
From slopes that the tide-stream hath sapped;
And sweeter than all that we call so
The seal of their slumber shall be
Till the graves that embosom them also
Be sapped of the sea.

II.

1.

For the heart of the waters is cruel,
And the kisses are dire of their lips,
And their waves are as fire is to fuel
To the strength of the sea-faring ships,
Though the sea's eye gleam as a jewel
To the sun's eye back as he dips.

2.

Though the sun's eye flash to the sea's
Live light of delight and of laughter,
And her lips breathe back to the breeze
The kiss that the wind's lips waft her
From the sun that subsides, and sees
No gleam of the storm's dawn after.

3.

And the wastes of the wild sea-marches
Where the borderers are matched in their might—
Bleak fens that the sun's weight parches,
Dense waves that reject his light—
Change under the change-coloured arches
Of changeless morning and night

4.

The waves are as ranks enrolled
Too close for the storm to sever:
The fens lie naked and cold,
But their heart fails utterly never:
The lists are set from of old,
And the warfare endureth for ever.

III.

1.

Miles, and miles, and miles of desolation!
Leagues on leagues on leagues without a change!
Sign or token of some eldest nation
Here would make the strange land not so strange.
Time-forgotten, yea since time's creation,
Seem these borders where the sea-birds range.

2.

Slowly, gladly, full of peace and wonder
Grows his heart who journeys here alone.
Earth and all its thoughts of earth sink under
Deep as deep in water sinks a stone.
Hardly knows it if the rollers thunder,
Hardly whence the lonely wind is blown.

3.

Tall the plumage of the rush-flower tosses,
Sharp and soft in many a curve and line
Gleam and glow the sea-coloured marsh-mosses,
Salt and splendid from the circling brine.
Streak on streak of glimmering seashine crosses
All the land sea-saturate as with wine.

4.

Far, and far between, in divers orders,
Clear grey steeples cleave the low grey sky;
Fast and firm as time-unshaken warders,
Hearts made sure by faith, by hope made high.
These alone in all the wild sea-borders
Fear no blast of days and nights that die.

5.

All the land is like as one man's face is,
Pale and troubled still with change of cares.
Doubt and death pervade her clouded spaces:
Strength and length of life and peace are theirs;
Theirs alone amid these weary places.
Seeing not how the wild world frets and fares.

6.

Firm and fast where all is cloud that changes
Cloud-clogged sunlight, cloud by sunlight thinned,
Stern and sweet, above the sand-hill ranges
Watch the towers and tombs of men that sinned
Once, now calm as earth whose only change is
Wind, and light, and wind, and cloud, and wind.

7.

Out and in and out the sharp straits wander,
In and out and in the wild way strives,
Starred and paved and lined with flowers that squander
Gold as golden as the gold of hives,
Salt and moist and multiform: but yonder,
See, what sign of life or death survives?

8.

Seen then only when the songs of olden
Harps were young whose echoes yet endure,
Hymned of Homer when his years were golden,
Known of only when the world was pure,
Here is Hades, manifest, beholden,
Surely, surely here, if aught be sure!

9.

Where the border-line was crossed, that, sundering
Death from life, keeps weariness from rest,
None can tell, who fares here forward wondering;
None may doubt but here might end his quest.
Here life's lightning joys and woes once thundering
Sea-like round him cease like storm suppressed.

10.

Here the wise wave-wandering steadfast-hearted
Guest of many a lord of many a land
Saw the shape or shade of years departed,

Saw the semblance risen and hard at hand,
Saw the mother long from love's reach parted,
Anticleia, like a statue stand.

11.

Statue? nay, nor tissued image woven
Fair on hangings in his father's hall;
Nay, too fast her faith of heart was proven,
Far too firm her loveliest love of all;
Love wherethrough the loving heart was cloven,
Love that hears not when the loud Fates call.

12.

Love that lives and stands up re-created
Then when life has ebbed and anguish fled;
Love more strong than death or all things fated,
Child's and mother's, lit by love and led;
Love that found what life so long awaited
Here, when life came down among the dead.

13.

Here, where never came alive another,
Came her son across the sundering tide
Crossed before by many a warrior brother
Once that warred on Ilion at his side;
Here spread forth vain hands to clasp the mother
Dead, that sorrowing for his love's sake died.

14.

Parted, though by narrowest of divisions,
Clasp he might not, only might implore,
Sundered yet by bitterest of derisions,
Son, and mother from the son she bore—
Here? But all dispeopled here of visions
Lies, forlorn of shadows even, the shore.

15.

All too sweet such men's Hellenic speech is,
All too fain they lived of light to see,
Once to see the darkness of these beaches,
Once to sing this Hades found of me
Ghostless, all its gulfs and creeks and reaches,
Sky, and shore, and cloud, and waste, and sea.

IV.

1.

But aloft and afront of me faring
Far forward as folk in a dream
That strive, between doubting and daring
Right on till the goal for them gleam,
Full forth till their goal on them lighten,
The harbour where fain they would be,
What headlands there darken and brighten?
What change in the sea?

2.

What houses and woodlands that nestle
Safe inland to lee of the hill
As it slopes from the headlands that wrestle
And succumb to the strong sea's will?
Truce is not, nor respite, nor pity,
For the battle is waged not of hands
Where over the grave of a city
The ghost of it stands.

3.

Where the wings of the sea-wind slacken,
Green lawns to the landward thrive,
Fields brighten and pine-woods blacken,
And the heat in their heart is alive;
They blossom and warble and murmur,
For the sense of their spirit is free:
But harder to shoreward and firmer
The grasp of the sea.

4.

Like ashes the low cliffs crumble,
The banks drop down into dust,
The heights of the hills are made humble,
As a reed's is the strength of their trust:
As a city's that armies environ,
The strength of their stay is of sand:
But the grasp of the sea is as iron,
Laid hard on the land.

5.

A land that is thirstier than ruin;
A sea that is hungrier than death;
Heaped hills that a tree never grew in;
Wide sands where the wave draws breath;
All solace is here for the spirit
That ever for ever may be
For the soul of thy son to inherit,
My mother, my sea.

6.

O delight of the headlands and beaches!
O desire of the wind on the wold,
More glad than a man's when it reaches
That end which it sought from of old
And the palm of possession is dreary
To the sense that in search of it sinned;
But nor satisfied ever nor weary
Is ever the wind.

7.

The delight that he takes but in living
Is more than of all things that live:
For the world that has all things for giving
Has nothing so goodly to give:
But more than delight his desire is,
For the goal where his pinions would be
Is immortal as air or as fire is,
Immense as the sea.

8.

Though hence come the moan that he borrows
From darkness and depth of the night,
Though hence be the spring of his sorrows,
Hence too is the joy of his might;
The delight that his doom is for ever
To seek and desire and rejoice,
And the sense that eternity never
Shall silence his voice.

9.

That satiety never may stifle
Nor weariness ever estrange

Nor time be so strong as to rifle
Nor change be so great as to change
His gift that renews in the giving.
The joy that exalts him to be
Alone of all elements living
The lord of the sea.

10.

What is fire, that its flame should consume her?
More fierce than all fires are her waves:
What is earth, that its gulfs should entomb her?
More deep are her own than their graves.
Life shrinks from his pinions that cover
The darkness by thunders bedinned:
But she knows him, her lord and her lover,
The godhead of wind.

11.

For a season his wings are about her,
His breath on her lips for a space;
Such rapture he wins not without her
In the width of his worldwide race.
Though the forests bow down, and the mountains
Wax dark, and the tribes of them flee,
His delight is more deep in the fountains
And springs of the sea.

12.

There are those too of mortals that love him,
There are souls that desire and require,
Be the glories of midnight above him
Or beneath him the daysprings of fire:
And their hearts are as harps that approve him
And praise him as chords of a lyre
That were fain with their music to move him
To meet their desire.

13.

To descend through the darkness to grace them,
Till darkness were lovelier than light:
To encompass and grasp and embrace them,
Till their weakness were one with his might:
With the strength of his wings to caress them,
With the blast of his breath to set free;

With the mouths of his thunders to bless them
For sons of the sea.

14.

For these have the toil and the guerdon
That the wind has eternally: these
Have part in the boon and the burden
Of the sleepless unsatisfied breeze,
That finds not, but seeking rejoices
That possession can work him no wrong:
And the voice at the heart of their voice is
The sense of his song.

15.

For the wind's is their doom and their blessing;
To desire, and have always above
A possession beyond their possessing,
A love beyond reach of their love.
Green earth has her sons and her daughters,
And these have their guerdons; but we
Are the wind's and the sun's and the water's,
Elect of the sea.

V.

1.

For the sea too seeks and rejoices,
Gains and loses and gains,
And the joy of her heart's own choice is
As ours, and as ours are her pains:
As the thoughts of our hearts are her voices,
And as hers is the pulse of our veins.

2.

Her fields that know not of dearth
Nor lie for their fruit's sake fallow
Laugh large in the depth of their mirth
But inshore here in the shallow,
Embroiled with encumbrance of earth,
Their skirts are turbid and yellow.

3.

The grime of her greed is upon her,
The sign of her deed is her soil;
As the earth's is her own dishonour,
And corruption the crown of her toil:
She hath spoiled and devoured, and her honour
Is this, to be shamed by her spoil.

4.

But afar where pollution is none,
Nor ensign of strife nor endeavour,
Where her heart and the sun's are one,
And the soil of her sin comes never,
She is pure as the wind and the sun,
And her sweetness endureth for ever.

VI.

1.

Death, and change, and darkness everlasting,
Deaf, that hears not what the daystar saith,
Blind, past all remembrance and forecasting,
Dead, past memory that it once drew breath;
These, above the washing tides and wasting,
Reign, and rule this land of utter death.

2.

Change of change, darkness of darkness, hidden,
Very death of very death, begun
When none knows,—the knowledge is forbidden—
Self-begotten, self-proceeding, one,
Born, not made—abhorred, unchained, unchidden,
Night stands here defiant of the sun.

3.

Change of change, and death of death begotten,
Darkness born of darkness, one and three,
Ghostly godhead of a world forgotten,
Crowned with heaven, enthroned on land and sea,
Here, where earth with dead men's bones is rotten,
God of Time, thy likeness worships thee.

4.

Lo, thy likeness of thy desolation,
Shape and figure of thy might, O Lord,
Formless form, incarnate miscreation,
Served of all things living and abhorred;
Earth herself is here thine incarnation,
Time, of all things born on earth adored.

5.

All that worship thee are fearful of thee;
No man may not worship thee for fear:
Prayers nor curses prove not nor disprove thee,
Move nor change thee with our change of cheer:
All at last, though all abhorred thee, love thee,
God, the sceptre of whose throne is here.

6.

Here thy throne and sceptre of thy station,
Here the palace paven for thy feet;
Here thy sign from nation unto nation
Passed as watchword for thy guards to greet,
Guards that go before thine exaltation,
Ages, clothed with bitter years and sweet.

7.

Here, where sharp the sea-bird shrills his ditty,
Flickering flame-wise through the clear live calm,
Rose triumphal, crowning all a city,
Roofs exalted once with prayer and psalm,
Built of holy hands for holy pity,
Frank and fruitful as a sheltering palm.

8.

Church and hospice wrought in faultless fashion,
Hall and chancel bounteous and sublime,
Wide and sweet and glorious as compassion,
Filled and thrilled with force of choral chime,
Filled with spirit of prayer and thrilled with passion
Hailed a God more merciful than Time.

9.

Ah, less mighty, less than Time prevailing,
Shrunk, expelled, made nothing at his nod,
Less than clouds across the sea-line sailing,

Lies he, stricken by his master's rod.
'Where is man?' the cloister murmurs wailing;
Back the mute shrine thunders—'Where is God?'

10.

Here is all the end of all his glory—
Dust, and grass, and barren silent stones.
Dead, like him, one hollow tower and hoary
Naked in the sea-wind stands and moans,
Filled and thrilled with its perpetual story:
Here, where earth is dense with dead men's bones.

11.

Low and loud and long, a voice for ever,
Sounds the wind's clear story like a song.
Tomb from tomb the waves devouring sever,
Dust from dust as years relapse along;
Graves where men made sure to rest, and never
Lie dismantled by the seasons' wrong.

12.

Now displaced, devoured and desecrated,
Now by Time's hands darkly disinterred,
These poor dead that sleeping here awaited
Long the archangel's re-creating word,
Closed about with roofs and walls high-gated
Till the blast of judgment should be heard,

13.

Naked, shamed, cast out of consecration,
Corpse and coffin, yea the very graves,
Scoffed at, scattered, shaken from their station,
Spurned and scourged of wind and sea like slaves,
Desolate beyond man's desolation,
Shrink and sink into the waste of waves.

14.

Tombs, with bare white piteous bones protruded,
Shroudless, down the loose collapsing banks,
Crumble, from their constant place detruded,
That the sea devours and gives not thanks.
Graves where hope and prayer and sorrow brooded
Gape and slide and perish, ranks on ranks.

15.

Rows on rows and line by line they crumble,
They that thought for all time through to be.
Scarce a stone whereon a child might stumble
Breaks the grim field paced alone of me.
Earth, and man, and all their gods wax humble
Here, where Time brings pasture to the sea.

VII.

1.

But afar on the headland exalted,
But beyond in the curl of the bay,
From the depth of his dome deep-vaulted
Our father is lord of the day.
Our father and lord that we follow,
For deathless and ageless is he;
And his robe is the whole sky's hollow,
His sandal the sea.

2.

Where the horn of the headland is sharper,
And her green floor glitters with fire,
The sea has the sun for a harper,
The sun has the sea for a lyre.
The waves are a pavement of amber,
By the feet of the sea-winds trod
To receive in a god's presence-chamber
Our father, the God.

3.

Time, haggard and changeful and hoary,
Is master and God of the land:
But the air is fulfilled of the glory
That is shed from our lord's right hand.
O father of all of us ever,
All glory be only to thee
From heaven, that is void of thee never,
And earth, and the sea.

4.

O Sun, whereof all is beholden,
Behold now the shadow of this death,
This place of the sepulchres, olden
And emptied and vain as a breath.
The bloom of the bountiful heather
Laughs broadly beyond in thy light
As dawn, with her glories to gather,
At darkness and night.

5.

Though the Gods of the night lie rotten
And their honour be taken away
And the noise of their names forgotten,
Thou, Lord, art God of the day.
Thou art father and saviour and spirit,
O Sun, of the soul that is free
And hath grace of thy grace to inherit
Thine earth and thy sea.

6.

The hills and the sands and the beaches,
The waters adrift and afar,
The banks and the creeks and the reaches,
How glad of thee all these are!
The flowers, overflowing, overcrowded,
Are drunk with the mad wind's mirth:
The delight of thy coming unclouded
Makes music of earth.

7.

I, last least voice of her voices,
Give thanks that were mute in me long
To the soul in my soul that rejoices
For the song that is over my song.
Time gives what he gains for the giving
Or takes for his tribute of me;
My dreams to the wind ever-living,
My song to the sea.

Algernon Charles Swinburne was born at 7 Chester Street, Grosvenor Place, in London, on April 5th, 1837. He was the eldest of six children born to Captain Charles Henry Swinburne and Lady Jane Henrietta, daughter of the 3rd Earl of Ashburnham, a wealthy Northumbrian family.

Swinburne spent his early years at East Dene in Bonchurch, on the Isle of Wight. As a child, Swinburne was nervous and frail, but also imbued with a nervous energy and fearlessness almost to the point of recklessness.

He was schooled at Eton College from 1849 to 1853. It was here that he first began to write poetry. He excelled at languages and whilst still at Eton won first prizes in both French and Italian.

From Eton he moved to Oxford where he attended at Balliol College from 1856. Here he met friends to whom he became closely attached, among them Dante Gabriel Rossetti, William Morris and Edward Burne-Jones, who in 1857, were painting their Arthurian murals on the walls of the Oxford Union. At Oxford Swinburne was mentored by Benjamin Jowett, the master of Balliol College, who recognised his poetic talent and, intervening on his behalf, tried to keep him from being expelled when he celebrated the Italian patriot Orsini, and his failed attempt on the life of Napoleon III in 1858. Swinburne had to leave the Universcity for a few months due to this but returned in May, 1860 but never received a degree.

Summers were usually spent at Capheaton Hall in Northumberland, the house of his grandfather, Sir John Swinburne, 6th Baronet, who had a famous library and was himself President of the Literary and Philosophical Society in Newcastle upon Tyne.

Swinburne proudly considered himself a native of Northumberland and this is reflected in poems such as the intensely patriotic 'Northumberland' and 'Grace Darling'. He enjoyed riding across the moors and was, it was said, a daring horseman, as he moved 'through honeyed leagues of the northland border', as he remembered the Scottish border in his Recollections.

In the period from 1857 to 1860, Swinburne was one of a number of Pre-Raphaelite's who visited and became part of Lady Pauline Trevelyan's intellectual circle at Wallington Hall, a few miles west of Morpeth in Northumberland.

After leaving college, he moved to London and began his career in earnest as well as becoming a constant visitor to the Rossetti's house. To Rossetti Swinburne was his 'little Northumbrian friend', an affectionate reference to Swinburne's small stature—a mere five foot four. Whatever Swinburne lacked in height he made up for in poetic talent. However, with the burden of such great talent came the unveiling of a dark side that was to cause him pain and would, at times, threaten his very existence with all manner of self-inflicted pains through drink, drugs and sado-machoism.

In 1860 Swinburne published two verse dramas; The Queen Mother and Rosamond but it would not be until 1865 that Swinburne would achieve literary success with Atalanta in Calydon.

In 1861, Swinburne visited Menton on the French Riviera to recover from the effects of yet another period of excess use of alcohol, staying at the Villa Laurenti. From Menton, Swinburne then travelled on to Italy, where he journeyed widely.

After Elizabeth Rossetti's death from suicide in 1862, he and Rossetti moved to Tudor House at 16 Cheyne Walk in Chelsea. The stories that survive from his year with Rossetti are typical Swinburne. In one, Rossetti once had to tell him to keep down the noise — he and a boyfriend had been sliding naked down the bannisters and disturbing Rossetti's painting. He took a sardonic delight in what the critic and biographer, Cecil Lang, calls "Algernonic exaggeration": When people began to talk scathingly about his homosexuality and other sexual proclivities, he circulated a story that he had engaged in pederasty and bestiality with a monkey — and then eaten it. How many of the stories were true and how many invented is unclear. Oscar Wilde called him "a braggart in matters of vice, who had done everything he could to convince his fellow citizens of his homosexuality and bestiality without being in the slightest degree a homosexual or a bestialiser."

In December 1862, Swinburne accompanied Scott and his guests on a trip to Tynemouth. Scott writes in his memoirs that, as they walked by the sea, Swinburne declaimed the as yet unpublished 'Hymn to Proserpine' and 'Laus Veneris' in his lilting intonation, while the waves 'were running the whole length of the long level sands towards Cullercoats and sounding like far-off acclamations'.

Swinburne possessed a curious combination of frail health and strength. He was small and slightly built, but an excellent swimmer and the first to climb Culver Cliff on the Isle of Wight. He had an extremely excitable disposition: people who met him described him as a "demoniac boy" who would go skipping about the room declaiming poetry at the top of his voice. In this as in many things, moderation was not the standard for him. Excess was. Once or twice he had fits, thought to be epileptic, in public; but he made this condition much worse by drinking past excess to unconsciousness. More than once he was delivered to the door in the small of the night, dead drunk. Throughout the 1860s and '70s he rode an alcoholic cycle of dissolution, collapse, drying out at home in the country, then returning to London where he would begin the cycle all over again.

His mania for masochism, particularly flagellation, most probably started in early childhood at Eton and was encouraged by his later friendships with Richard Monckton Milnes (one of Tennyson's fellow Apostles), who introduced him to the works of the Marquis de Sade, and Richard Burton, the Victorian explorer and adventurer. Swinburne was an alcoholic and algolagniac (a desire for sexual gratification through inflicting pain on oneself or others; sadomasochism). He found life difficult, unfulfilling but still his poetic talents pushed to the fore.

Although Swinburne continued to publish some works in periodicals in 1865 he was granted recognition by both public and critics with Atalanta in Calydon written in the style of a classical Greek tragedy.

There followed "Laus Veneris" and Poems and Ballads (1866), with their sexually charged passages, absolutely decadent for polite Victorian society, which were attacked all the more violently as a result. The poems written in homage of Sappho of Lesbos such as "Anactoria" and "Sapphics" were especially savaged. The volume also contained poems such as "The Leper," "Laus Veneris," and "St Dorothy" which evoke both Swinburne's and a general Victorian fascination with the Middle Ages, and are explicitly mediaeval in style, tone and construction. With its publication came instant notoriety. He was now identified with indecent and decadent themes and the precept of art for art's sake.

Swinburne's meeting in 1867 with his long-time hero Mazzini, the Italian patriot living in England in exile, was the beginning of a poetical journey that now became more serious and more engaged with serious thought, initially leading to the political poems in the volume Songs Before Sunrise.

Also in 1867 he was introduced to Adah Isaacs Menken, the American actress, poet and circus rider, whose main fame seemed to be riding naked on a horse (in fact she wore tight nude coloured clothing) for her performance in the melodrama Mazeppa (itself based on a poem by Lord Byron). Although they had a short affair Adah's quote implies that Swinburne was not ready for a relationship that did not involve some self-sabotage; "I can't make him understand that biting's no use."

In 1879, with Swinburne nearly dead from alcoholism and dissolution, his legal advisor Theodore Watts-Dunton took him in, and was gradually successful in getting him to adapt to a healthier lifestyle. Swinburne lived the rest of his life at Watts-Dunton's house. He saw less and less of his old bohemian friends, who thought him a prisoner at The Pines, but his growing deafness also accounts for some of his decreased sociability. By now Swinburne was 42, and was moving from a young man of rebelliousness to a figure of social respectability. It was said of Watts-Dunton that he saved the man and killed the poet.

It is clear that Swinburne had an addictive personality, and clearly incapable of moderation in his pursuit of any chosen vices. This, of course, would both nourish and perhaps sabotage his poetic career. His poetry follows the somewhat clichéd pattern of early flourish and later decline; indeed some of the fresher pieces in the second and third series of Poems and Ballads (published in 1878 and 1889) were actually written during his days at Oxford. Nevertheless, his last collection, A Channel Passage, has some beautiful poems, including "The Lake of Gaube."

He is best remembered as the supreme technician in metre, with a versatility which exceeds even Tennyson's, but which lacks a corresponding emotional range. His obsessions are not widely enough shared; and if he cannot shock us by the strangeness of his desires nor the shrillness of his anti-theistical exclamations, often what remains is not enough to fully engage with the audience.

Swinburne is considered a poet of the decadent school, although he perhaps professed to more vice than he actually indulged in to advertise his deviance. Common gossip of the time reported that he also had a deep crush on the explorer Sir Richard Francis Burton, despite the fact that Swinburne himself abhorred travel. Fact and fiction are easily absorbed by the other so are difficult to untangle even now.

Many critics consider his mastery of vocabulary, rhyme and metre impressive, although he has also been criticised for his florid style and word choices that only fit the rhyme scheme rather than contributing to the meaning of the piece. A. E. Housman, although a critic, had great praise for his rhyming ability: to Swinburne the sonnet was child's play: the task of providing four rhymes was not hard enough, and he wrote long poems in which each stanza required eight or ten rhymes, and wrote them so that he never seemed to be saying anything for the rhyme's sake.

Throughout his career Swinburne published literary criticism of great worth. His deep knowledge of world literatures contributed to a critical style rich in quotation, allusion, and comparison. He is particularly noted for discerning studies of Elizabethan dramatists and of many English and French poets and novelists. As well he was a noted essayist and wrote two novels.

Swinburne was nominated for the Nobel Prize in Literature every year from 1903 to 1907 and then again in 1909.

H.P. Lovecraft, the master of the dark side and a decent poet himself, considered Swinburne "the only real poet in either England or America after the death of Mr. Edgar Allan Poe."

Swinburne was also responsible for devising a poetic form called the roundel, a variation of the French Rondeau form. In 1883 he published A Century of Roundels with several of the roundels dedicated to Dante's sister, the poet Christina Georgina Rossetti. Swinburne wrote to Edward Burne-Jones in 1883: "I have got a tiny new book of songs or songlets, in one form and all manner of metres ... just coming out, of which Miss Rossetti has accepted the dedication. I hope you and Georgie [his wife Georgiana] will find something to like among a hundred poems of nine lines each, twenty-four of which are about babies or small children".

Opinions of the Roundel poems move between those who find them captivating and brilliant, to others who find them merely clever and contrived. One of them, A Baby's Death, was set to music by the English composer Sir Edward Elgar as the song "Roundel: The little eyes that never knew Light".

After the first Poems and Ballads, Swinburne's later poetry was devoted more to philosophy and politics, including the unification of Italy, particularly in the volume Songs before Sunrise. He did not stop writing love poetry entirely, indeed it was only in 1882 that his great epic-length poem, Tristram of Lyonesse, was published, its contents lyrical rather than shocking. His versification, and especially his rhyming technique, remain of high quality to the end.

Algernon Charles Swinburne died of influenza, at the Pines in London on April 10th, 1909 at the age of 72. He was buried at St. Boniface Church, Bonchurch on the Isle of Wight.

Algernon Charles Swinburne – A Concise Bibliography

Verse Drama
The Queen Mother (1860)
Rosamond (1860)
Chastelard (1865)
Bothwell (1874)
Mary Stuart (1881)
Marino Faliero (1885)
Locrine (1887)
The Sisters (1892)
Rosamund, Queen of the Lombards (1899)

Poetry
Atalanta in Calydon (1865)*
Poems and Ballads (1866)
Songs Before Sunrise (1871)
Songs of Two Nations (1875)
Erechtheus (1876)*
Poems and Ballads, Second Series (1878)
Songs of the Springtides (1880)
Studies in Song (1880)
The Heptalogia, or the Seven against Sense. A Cap with Seven Bells (1880)
Tristram of Lyonesse (1882)
A Dark Month & Other Poems

A Century of Roundels (1883)
A Midsummer Holiday and Other Poems (1884)
Poems and Ballads, Third Series (1889)
Astrophel and Other Poems (1894)
The Tale of Balen (1896)
A Channel Passage and Other Poems (1904)

*Although formally tragedies, Atlanta in Calydon and Erechtheus are traditionally included with his poetry.

Criticism
William Blake: A Critical Essay (1868, new edition 1906)
Under the Microscope (1872)
George Chapman: A Critical Essay (1875)
Essays and Studies (1875)
A Note on Charlotte Brontë (1877)
A Study of Shakespeare (1880)
A Study of Victor Hugo (1886)
A Study of Ben Johnson (1889)
Studies in Prose and Poetry (1894)
The Age of Shakespeare (1908)
Shakespeare (1909)

Major Collections
The Poems of Algernon Charles Swinburne, 6 vols. 1904.
The Tragedies of Algernon Charles Swinburne, 5 vols. 1905.
The Complete Works of Algernon Charles Swinburne, 20 vols. Bonchurch Edition. 1925-7.
The Swinburne Letters, 6 vols. 1959-62.

www.ingramcontent.com/pod-product-compliance
Lightning Source LLC
Chambersburg PA
CBHW060051050426
42448CB00011B/2407